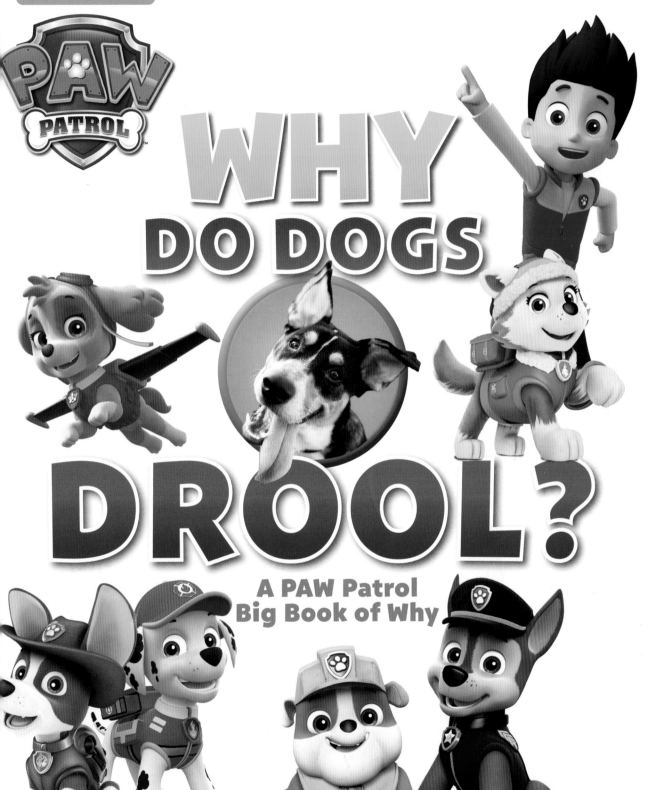

WHY DO DOGS DROOL?

A PAW Patrol Big Book of Why

Why is the sky blue?

Our air is filled with lots of tiny particles of dust as well as gases that we can't see, such as oxygen. All different colors of light bounce off of these tiny bits, but blue bounces off the best! That's why the sky looks blue.

Let's take to the sky!

Puppy Punchlines

Why did the pups tell the sky to cheer up?

Because it seemed a bit blue!

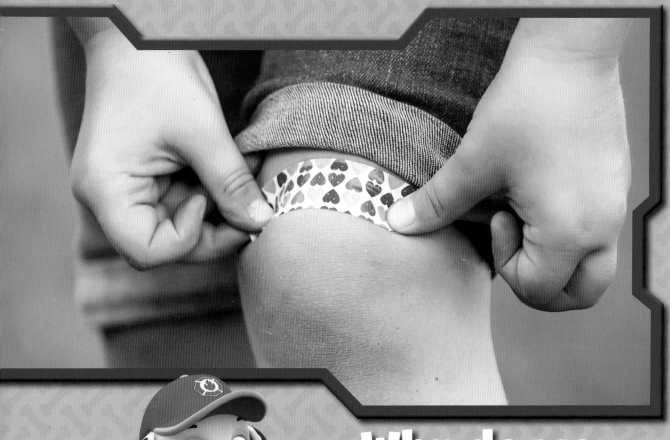

Why do we put bandages on cuts?

To keep out germs! Bandages help a cut stay clean, so if you get a cut somewhere that might get dirty easily (like your hand), it's a good idea to use a bandage. Make sure to change it every day!

Need a bandage? I'm here to help!

Why doesn't it hurt to get a haircut?

Because your hair isn't alive! It's made of something called keratin *(care-a-tin)*. Only the root of your hair is alive—that's why it hurts to pluck out your hair, but not to trim it.

I love getting a bath at Katie's Pet Parlor!

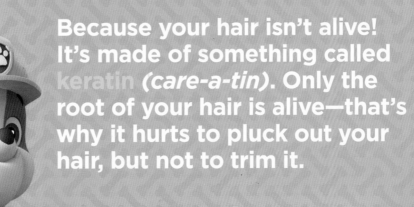

Did You Know?

Your nails are made of keratin, too! That's why it doesn't hurt to trim the white parts.

Why do lions roar?

Lions roar to talk with one another, like when a mother lion roars to call to her cubs. When a lion roars really loudly, he's warning other animals that they're on his territory!

Lions roar super loud!

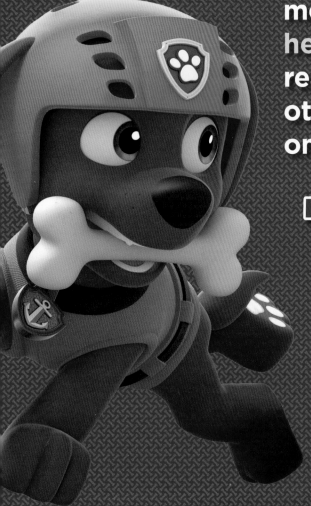

Did You Know?
A group of lions is called a pride!

Why do balloons float?

Balloons that float are filled with helium, a gas that's even lighter than air. Lighter gases always rise above heavier gases. That's why helium floats!

This pup's gotta fly!

Why do boats float?

Boats float because they're buoyant *(boy-ant)*! That means when they push their weight down on the water, the water pushes back up, keeping the boat above the waves. The shape of a boat also helps it float. Lots of big boats have flat bottoms because it gives the water more space to push up against.

Ready, set, get wet...and float!

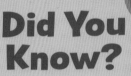

Did You Know?
Objects filled with air also float in water!

Why do caterpillars make cocoons?

So they can become butterflies! Caterpillars go through a process called metamorphosis (met-ah-morf-oh-sis). They hang upside down on twigs or branches and build cocoons around themselves. While they're in the cocoons, they grow wings and transform into butterflies.

Did You Know?

Butterflies learn how to fly in just a few hours!

Flying in just a few hours? That's brave!

Why do we lose baby teeth?

To make room for our adult teeth! Our mouths don't have room for all our adult teeth until we've grown up a bit, so our baby teeth are there to save their place.

Pups lose their first teeth, too! I remember when I did.

Did You Know?

Children have 20 teeth and adults have 32!

Chickaletta doesn't need to fly—she always rides in my purse!

Why don't chickens fly like other birds?

Chickens do fly, but they can only fly for a few feet before coming back down because their wings are too small!

Why do dogs lick people?

There are lots of reasons a dog will lick you. For one thing, the dog probably thinks you taste good! Most people's skin is usually a little salty.

Aww, thanks Chase!

Puppy Punchlines
What do you call a panting pooch?
A hot dog!

Dogs also lick people to try to communicate that they need something (maybe more water or to go outside) or just to show love!

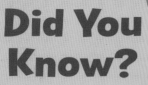

Did You Know?

Some islands are naturally formed, and some are made by people!

Why don't islands sink?

Because they're connected to the Earth underwater! Some islands are the tops of mountains that are mostly underwater, and some islands are created when wind and water wear away the land around them.

I like my house high and dry!

Why does it snow?

Air is full of tiny bits of water called vapor. When enough vapor collects, it makes rain. But when it's really cold, the vapor freezes and forms snow!

Ice or snow, I'm ready to go!

Why do penguins waddle?

Penguins waddle because they have short legs and big feet! It's the easiest way for them to walk around on land. If they want to go faster, they can slide on their bellies!

I was born to slide!

Why does the sun set?

The sun doesn't really set or rise—it just looks like it does because the way the Earth moves! Our world slowly spins around, making a full rotation every 24 hours. When your part of the world rotates past the sun, it makes it look like the sun is setting.

Did You Know?

When the Earth turns enough to see the sun again, it looks like the sun is rising high in the sky!

Why do astronauts float?

Because there's less gravity in outer space! Gravity is the force that holds things or make them fall to the ground. People in outer space are so far away from Earth that the gravity doesn't affect them as much.

Astronauts are amazing space heroes!

Polar bear fur is super warm for the *ruff-ruff* wintery weather!

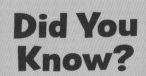
Why do polar bears have white fur?

Actually, a polar bear's fur isn't white—it's transparent! That means it's see-through! It just looks white because of the way light bounces off of it. Scientists think polar bears have this fur to blend in better with their snowy environment.

Why do cows wear bells?

Cows wear bells to make it easy for their owners to find them! If a farmer doesn't see her cow right away, she can just listen for the bell.

Bettina wears a bell. That way I can hear her when she's on the moooo-ve!

Why do pigs roll in mud?

Pigs don't sweat, so they use mud to stay cool! On a hot day, taking a dip in the mud can cool off a pig even more than water.

I think I'd rather take a swim!

Why do turtles have shells?

For protection! Turtles have hard shells to keep them safe from predators. Scientists also think that turtles developed shells to help them burrow into the ground.

It's like being in a submarine all the time!

Why do cats have whiskers?

A cat's whiskers are super sensitive! It's like an extra sense. They help cats determine whether or not they can fit in a small space and even help them move around in the dark.

Why do dogs drool?

Dogs have saliva (also known as spit) for the same reason people do: to help them swallow and digest food. If a dog has droopy lips, like a basset hound, it might drip more saliva than most dogs and look like it's drooling!

You deserve a treat!

No question
is too BIG,

NO PUP
is too small!

Media Lab Books
For inquiries, call 646-838-6637

Copyright 2017 Topix Media Lab

Published by Topix Media Lab
14 Wall Street, Suite 4B
New York, NY 10005

Printed in China

ISBN-10: 1-942556-83-7
ISBN-13: 978-1942556-83-1

CEO Tony Romando

Vice President of Brand Marketing Joy Bomba
Director of Finance Vandana Patel
Director of Sales and New Markets Tom Mifsud
Manufacturing Director Nancy Puskuldjian
Financial Analyst Matthew Quinn
Brand Marketing Assistant Taylor Hamilton

Editor-in-Chief Jeff Ashworth
Creative Director Steven Charny
Photo Director Dave Weiss
Managing Editor Courtney Kerrigan
Senior Editors Tim Baker, James Ellis

Content Editor Kaytie Norman
Content Designer Rebecca Stone
Content Photo Editor Catherine Armanasco
Art Director Susan Dazzo
Assistant Managing Editor Holland Baker
Senior Designer Michelle Lock
Designer Danielle Santucci
Assistant Photo Editor Jessica Ariel Wendroff
Assistant Editors Trevor Courneen, Alicia Kort
Editorial Assistants Mira Braneck, Brendan Luke,
Rachel Philips, Jordan Reisman

Co-Founders Bob Lee, Tony Romando

Shutterstock: cover, p9, 10, 15, 17, 18, 19, 20, 21, 22, 26, 28, 29; p2 urbancow/iStock; p4 emholk/iStock; p5 ArtisticCaptures/iStock; p7
skynesher/iStock; p8 ideabug/iStock; p12 andipantz/iStock; p13 akarelias/iStock; p16 yykkaa/iStock; p24 Andrew Cole/Alamy; p25
taviphoto/iStock

1C G17 1